Why and
How Sho
I Tell Others?

Booklets taken from Questions of Life:

Is There More to Life Than This?

Who Is Jesus?

Why Did Jesus Die?

How Can We Have Faith?

Why and How Do I Pray?

Why and How Should I Read the Bible?

How Does God Guide Us?

The Holy Spirit

How Can I Resist Evil?

Why and How Should I Tell Others?

Does God Heal Today?

What About the Church?

How Can I Make the Most of the Rest of My Life?

Why and How Should I Tell Others?

NICKY GUMBEL

First published 1993
Revised in 2011
This new edition 2016

10 09 08 07 06 05 04 03 02 01

ISBN: 978 1 909309 69 2

Published by Alpha International
Holy Trinity Brompton
Brompton Road
London SW7 1JA
Email: publications@alpha.org

Illustrated by Charlie Mackesy

Alpha

Alpha is a practical introduction to the Christian faith, initiated by HTB in London and now being run by thousands of churches, of many denominations, throughout the world. If you are interested in finding out more about the Christian faith and would like details of your nearest Alpha, please visit our website:

alpha.org

or contact:
The Alpha Office,
HTB Brompton Road,
London,
SW7 1JA

Tel: 0845 644 7544

Alpha titles available

Why Jesus? A booklet – given to all participants at the start of Alpha. 'The clearest, best illustrated and most challenging short presentation of Jesus that I know.' – Michael Green

Why Christmas? The Christmas version of *Why Jesus?*

Questions of Life Alpha in book form. In fifteen compelling chapters Nicky Gumbel points the way to an authentic Christianity which is exciting and relevant to today's world.

Searching Issues The seven issues most often raised by participants on Alpha, including, suffering, other religions, science and Christianity, and the Trinity.

A Life Worth Living What happens after Alpha? Based on the book of Philippians, this is an invaluable next step for those who have just completed Alpha, and for anyone eager to put their faith on a firm biblical footing.

Contents

Why and How Should
I Tell Others?

I used to be rather irritated by Christians who tried to tell me about their faith. My reaction was, 'I am an atheist, but I don't go around trying to make atheists of other people'. It seemed to me interfering. Why should Christians talk about their faith?

"I happen to believe in chocolate, but I eat it quietly, alone, in my own room"

Isn't it a private matter? Isn't the best sort of Christian the one who just lives the Christian life? Sometimes people say to me, 'I have a good friend who is a devout Christian. They have a really strong faith – but they do not talk about it. Isn't that the highest form of Christianity?'

The short answer is that someone must have told *them* about the Christian faith. If the early Christians hadn't told people about Jesus, none of us today would know about him. The longer answer is that there are good reasons for telling others about Jesus. First, it is a command of Jesus himself. Tom Forrest, the Roman Catholic priest who first suggested to the Pope the idea of calling the 1990s 'The Decade of Evangelism', points out that the word 'go' appears 1,514 times in the Bible (RSV), 233 times in the New Testament and 54 times in Matthew's Gospel. Jesus tells us to 'go':

> 'Go to the lost sheep…'
> 'Go and tell…'
> 'Go and invite all you meet…'
> 'Go and make disciples…'

Indeed, these are the last recorded words of Jesus in Matthew's Gospel:

> Then Jesus came to them and said, 'All authority in heaven and on earth has been given to me. Therefore go and make disciples of all nations, baptising them in the name of

the Father and of the Son and of the Holy
Spirit, and teaching them to obey everything I
have commanded you. And surely I will be with
you always, to the very end of the age'.
Matthew 28:18–20

Second, we tell people because of our love for others.
If we were in the Sahara Desert and had discovered
an oasis, it would be extremely selfish not to tell
the people around us who were thirsty where their
thirst could be satisfied. Jesus is the only one who can
satisfy the thirsty hearts of men and women. Often
the recognition of this thirst comes from surprising
sources. The singer Sinead O'Connor said in an
interview: 'As a race we feel empty. This is because our
spirituality has been wiped out and we don't know how
to express ourselves. As a result we're encouraged to fill
that gap with alcohol, drugs, sex or money. People out
there are screaming for the truth.'

Third, we tell others because, having discovered the
good news ourselves, we feel an urgent desire to pass
it on. If we have received good news we want to tell
other people. When our first child was born, we had a
list of about ten people to ring first. Top of the list was
Pippa's mother. I told her that we had a son and that he
and Pippa were well. I then tried ringing my mother,
but the phone was engaged. The third person on the
list was Pippa's sister. By the time I had telephoned her

she had already heard the news from Pippa's mother and so had all the others on the list. My mother's phone had been engaged because Pippa's mother was ringing her with the news. Good news travels fast. I did not need to implore Pippa's mother to pass on the message. She was bursting to tell them all. When we are excited about our relationship with Jesus, it is the most natural thing in the world to want to tell people.

"I know you're only a postbox, but you need to know about Jesus"

But how do we go about telling others? It seems to me that there are two opposite dangers. First, there is the danger of insensitivity. When I first became a

Christian I fell into this. I was so excited about what had happened that I longed for everyone else to follow suit. After I had been a Christian for a few days, I went to a party determined to tell everyone. I saw a friend dancing and decided the first step was to make her realise her need for God. So I went up to her and said, 'You look awful. You really need Jesus.' She thought that I had gone mad. It was not the most effective way of telling someone the good news! (However, she did later become a Christian, quite independently of me, and she is now my wife!).

The next party I went to, I decided to go well equipped. I got hold of a number of booklets, Christian books on various issues and a New Testament. I stuffed them into every pocket I could find. Somehow I managed to find a girl who was willing to dance with me. It was hard going with so many books in my pockets, so I asked if we could sit down. I soon brought the subject round to Christianity. For every question she asked, I was able to produce a book from my pocket on exactly that subject. Eventually she went away with an armful of books. The next day she was going to France and was reading one of the books I had given her on the boat. Suddenly she understood the truth of what Jesus had done for her and, turning to her neighbour, she said, 'I have just become a Christian.' A few years later, tragically, she died in a riding accident at the age of twenty-one. Even though I didn't go about it in quite the right way, it was wonderful that she had come to Christ before she died.

If we charge around like a bull in a china shop, sooner or later we get hurt. Even if we approach the subject sensitively, we may still get hurt. When we do, we tend to withdraw. Certainly this was my experience. After a few years, I moved from the danger of insensitivity and fell into the opposite danger of fear. There was a time (ironically, it was when I was at theological college) when I became fearful of even talking about Jesus to those who were not Christians. On one occasion, a group of us went from the college to a parish mission on the outskirts of Liverpool, to tell people the good news. Each night we had supper with different people from the parish. One night, a friend of mine called Rupert and I were sent to supper with a couple who were on the fringe of the church (or, to be more accurate, the wife was on the fringe, and the husband was not a churchgoer). Halfway through the main course the husband asked me what we were doing up there. I stumbled, stammered, hesitated and prevaricated. He kept on repeating the question. Eventually Rupert said straight out, 'We have come here to tell people about Jesus.' I felt deeply embarrassed and hoped the ground would swallow us all up! I realised how frozen with fear I had become, and that I was afraid to even utter the word 'Jesus'.

In order to avoid these dangers of insensitivity and fear, we need to realise that telling others about Jesus arises out of our own relationship with God. It is a natural part of that relationship. I find it helpful to think of this subject under five headings – all beginning with the letter 'p': presence, persuasion, proclamation, power and prayer.

Presence

Jesus said to his disciples:

> You are the salt of the earth. But if the salt loses its saltiness, how can it be made salty again? It is no longer good for anything, except to be thrown out and trampled under foot. You are the light of the world. A city on a hill cannot be hidden. Neither do people light a lamp and put it under a bowl. Instead they put it on its stand, and it gives light to everyone in the house. In the same way, let your light shine

> before others, that they may see your good
> deeds and praise your Father in heaven.
> Matthew 5:13–16

Jesus calls us to have a wide-ranging influence ('salt of the *earth*' and 'the light of the *world*'). In order to exercise this influence we need to be 'in the world' (at work, where we live, and among our family and friends) and not withdrawn from it. Yet we are called to be different – to live as followers of Christ in the world, so that we can be effective as salt and light in it.

In the ancient world, without refrigeration, salt was used to keep meat wholesome and to prevent it from rotting. As Christians, we are called to stop society going bad. We do this as we speak out about moral and social issues and as we work to alleviate poverty and inequality.

Second, Jesus calls us to be light, and he reminds us that it's no good covering a lamp. How do we light up the world? By our good deeds, says Jesus; by everything we do as Christians.

Living out the Christian life is the most appropriate way of passing on the good news to those who live in very close proximity to us. This certainly applies to our family, work colleagues and those we live with.

When I first became a Christian, I immediately tried to convert my parents. But I then realised that this was counter-productive. A friend pointed out that to declare to my parents, 'I've become a Christian', was an implied criticism of how they had brought me up. Continually speaking about our faith may backfire. People are more likely to be affected by genuine love and concern – by living out the Christian faith. Similarly, at work people should notice our consistency, honesty, truthfulness, hard work, reliability, refusal to gossip and desire to encourage other people.

This is of great importance if one's husband or wife is not a Christian. Peter encouraged Christian wives that if any of them have husbands who 'do not believe the word, they may be won over *without words* by the behaviour of their wives, when they see the purity and reverence of your lives' (1 Peter 3:1–2, italics mine).

Bruce and Geraldine Streather were married in December 1973. When Geraldine became a Christian in 1981, Bruce was not remotely interested. He was a busy lawyer and most weekends he used to play golf, rather than go to church.

For ten years Geraldine prayed for him and lived the Christian life at home as best she could. She did not put any pressure on him. Over the years, Bruce was struck by her kindness and consideration, especially to his mother whose cancer and related illnesses made their life increasingly difficult. Eventually, in 1991, she invited him to come to an Alpha celebration party. Bruce came, and decided to go on the following Alpha.

Geraldine wrote to me afterwards saying, 'I cried all the way home and prayed, telling God that as I had got Bruce to Alpha, he must do the rest. When Bruce returned from the first night, all I asked him was whether he had enjoyed himself.

On the seventh week of Alpha, Bruce gave his life to Christ and by the end he was one of the most enthusiastic Christians I have ever met. Her letter continued: 'At every dinner party we go to he talks to people about God and I'm left at the other end of the table listening to what he is saying. It seems that all my prayers have been answered.'

We are called to be salt and light, not just to our family and our immediate friends, but also to all the people around us. Sometimes we can struggle to see 'beyond the narrow confines of our own little worlds'. However, we are called to have compassion for those who are suffering. We can do this by getting involved in projects that relieve human need: hunger, homelessness, and poverty. We are also called to fight for social justice. We can do this by campaigning to abolish exploitation, inequality and inhumanity.

William Wilberforce was twenty-seven when he sensed God's call to fight against the inhuman, degrading slave trade. Ten million slaves left Africa for the plantations in 1787, and in 1789 he put down a motion in the House of Commons concerning the slave trade. It was not a popular cause, but he said this in his Abolition Speech: 'So enormous, so dreadful did its wickedness appear that my own mind was completely made up for abolition. Let the consequences be what they would; I from that time determined I would never rest until I had effected its abolition.'

Bills were debated in 1789, 1791, 1792, 1794, 1796, 1798, 1799 and they all failed. In 1831 he sent a message to the Anti-Slavery Society in which he said: 'Our motto must be perseverance, and ultimately I trust the Almighty will crown our efforts with success.' In July 1833 the Abolition of Slavery Bill was passed in both Houses of Parliament. Three days later Wilberforce died. He was buried in Westminster Abbey in national recognition of his forty-five years of persevering struggle on behalf of African slaves.

There are issues today that are on the same scale. More than 1.2 billion individuals are trapped in absolute poverty, a condition characterised by malnutrition, disease, squalor, infant mortality, and low life expectancy. At least a billion people live on less than a dollar a day and go to bed hungry every night. Every four seconds poverty takes a child's life. Every day, 17,000 children die of treatable diseases. In 2014, 790,000 adults and children died of AIDS in Sub-Saharan Africa – this accounted for 66 per cent of the world's AIDS death that year. There are 15 million preventable deaths each year. Slavery remains an issue in many parts of the world.

Bono, lead singer of the Irish rock band U2, was invited to address the Labour Party Conference in 2004. He spoke about his time working in an Ethiopian orphanage:

> The locals knew me as 'Dr Good Morning'. The children called me 'The Girl with the Beard'. Don't ask. [Ethiopia] just blew my mind; it opened my mind. On our last day at the orphanage a man handed me his baby and said, 'Take him with you.' He knew in Ireland his son would live; in Ethiopia his son would die. I turned him down. In that moment I started this journey. In that moment I became the worst thing of all: a rock-star with a cause. Except this isn't a cause – 6,500 Africans dying a day of treatable, preventable disease – dying for want of medicines you and I can get at our local chemist: that's not a cause; that's an emergency.[1]

It is easy to be overwhelmed by the scale of these problems and to think, 'Can we really make a difference?' Is there anything we can do as individuals?

One day a man was walking along a beach as the tide was receding. He saw tens of thousands of starfish stranded on the beach, drying out and slowly dying. He noticed a young boy picking up the starfish one at a time, and throwing them back into the sea. He approached the boy and said to him, 'With tens of thousands of those starfish lying up and down the beach you must feel like you're not making much of a difference.' As the boy tossed yet another starfish into the sea he turned to the man and said, 'I bet it made a difference to that one.'

In a similar way, we might not be able to solve all the problems in the world, but we can do something. Nelson Mandela said, 'It's not the kings and generals who make history, but the masses of the people.'

Having said this, being 'lights in the world' does not just involve our lifestyle; it also involves our lips. Our family, our friends and colleagues will eventually ask questions about our faith. Peter writes: 'Always be prepared to give an answer to everyone who asks you to give the reason for the hope that you have. But do this with gentleness and respect' (1 Peter 3:15).

When we do get opportunities to speak, how do we go about it?

Persuasion

Many people today have objections to the Christian faith or, at least, questions which they want answered before they are ready to come to faith in Christ. They need to be persuaded about the truth. Paul was willing to try to persuade people, because he loved them: 'Since, then, we know what it is to fear the Lord, we try to *persuade* people' (2 Corinthians 5:11, italics mine).

There is a big difference between persuasion and pressure. I, for one, run a mile if anyone tries to pressurise me to do anything. The effect of pressure is the opposite to that of persuasion. When Paul went to Thessalonica he 'reasoned', 'explained' and 'proved' from the Scriptures that the Christ had to suffer and rise from the dead: '... some of the Jews were persuaded...' (Acts 17:4). In Corinth, while making tents during the week, 'every Sabbath he reasoned in the synagogue, trying to persuade Jews and Greeks' (Acts 18:4).

During the course of conversations about the Christian faith, objections will often be raised and we need to be equipped to deal with these. On one occasion, Jesus was talking to a woman about the mess her life was in (John 4). Then he offered her eternal life. At that moment she raised a theological question about places of worship. He answered it, but quickly brought the conversation back to the essential issue. This is a good example for us to follow.

As well as being prepared to give an answer, we must also be prepared to listen to people, to understand where they are coming from. When I was struggling with the Christian faith, I did have intellectual objections. However, I was also beginning to realise the implications that becoming a Christian might have on my lifestyle. I was even worried that, since I had argued quite publicly at university against Christianity, I would lose face if I suddenly announced that I had become a Christian. There can, therefore, be other factors at work to which we need to be sensitive.

I am very grateful to the people who did help me to overcome my objections. When the crew first realised that the Titanic was sinking, they rushed around trying to persuade people to get into the lifeboats, but many passengers didn't believe them and wouldn't get in. Some of those early lifeboats went away half-empty. Yet the crew were trying to persuade them to get in out of love. Similarly, trying to persuade people about Christianity is an act of love.

Proclamation

The heart of telling others is the proclamation of the good news of Jesus Christ. There are many ways in which this can be done.

1. Come and see

One of the simplest and most effective ways is bringing people to hear the gospel explained by someone else. This can often be more advisable, especially in the early stages of our Christian lives, than trying to explain the gospel ourselves.

Many who come to faith in Christ have lots of friends who have little or no connection with the church. This provides an excellent opportunity to say to these friends, as Jesus did on one occasion, 'Come... and you will see' (John 1:39). A woman in her twenties became a Christian and started coming to church in London. At weekends, however, she would stay with her parents in Wiltshire, and then she insisted on leaving them at 3 pm on Sunday afternoon in order to make it to church. One Sunday evening she got stuck in a bad traffic jam on the way into London and could not get to the evening service. She was so upset that she burst into tears. She went round to see some friends, who did not even know she had become a Christian. They asked her what was wrong. She answered through the tears, 'I've missed church.' They were totally mystified. The next Sunday they all came to see what they were missing! One of them became a Christian very shortly afterwards.

There is no higher privilege and no greater joy than enabling someone to find out about Jesus Christ. The former Archbishop of Canterbury, William Temple, wrote a commentary on John's Gospel. When he came to the words, 'And he [Andrew] brought Simon to Jesus', he wrote a short but momentous sentence: 'The greatest service that one man can render another.'

We don't hear much more about Andrew except that he was always bringing people to Jesus (John 6:8; 12:22). But Simon Peter, his brother, went on to be one of the greatest influences in the history of Christianity. We cannot all be Simon Peters, but we can all do what Andrew did – we can bring someone to Jesus.

Albert McMakin was a 24-year-old farmer who had recently come to faith in Christ. He was so full of enthusiasm that he filled a van with people and took them to a meeting to hear about Jesus. There was a good-looking farmer's son whom he was especially keen to get to a meeting, but this young man was hard to persuade – he was busy falling in and out of love with different girls, and did not seem to be attracted to Christianity. Eventually, Albert McMakin managed to persuade him to come by asking him to drive the van. When they arrived, Albert's guest decided to go in, was 'spellbound' and began to have thoughts he had never known before. He went back again and again until one night, he went forward and gave his life to Jesus Christ. That man, the driver of the van, was Billy Graham. The year was 1934. Since then Billy Graham has spoken to 215 million people in person about the Christian faith. He has been the friend and confidant of ten American presidents. We cannot all be like Billy Graham, but we can all do what Albert McMakin did – we can all bring our friends to Jesus.

2. Tell our own story

One powerful way of communicating the gospel is to tell our own story. We see a biblical model in Paul's testimony in Acts 26:9–23. It falls into three parts: he speaks about what he was like before (vv.9–11), what it meant to meet Jesus (vv.12–15) and what it has meant for him since (vv.19–23).

When a blind man was healed by Jesus, many people came to question him about it, including the Pharisees who cross-examined him and tried to trap him. The blind man did not know how to answer all their questions but he knew what God had done: 'One thing I do know is I was blind but now I see!' (John 9:25). It is hard to argue with that.

3. Explain the gospel yourself

When explaining what someone has to do to become a Christian, a framework can be helpful. There are many different ways of presenting the gospel. I have set out the method I use in a booklet called *Why Jesus?* I then lead people in the prayer which you will find at the end of the booklet *How Can We Have Faith?*.

One man in our church told me about how he had come to Christ. He was going through difficulties in his business and had to go to the United States on a business trip. He was not feeling very happy as he rode in a taxi to the airport. On the dashboard of the taxi he noticed pictures of the taxi driver's children, so he asked him about his family. As they went on, he felt great love coming from the man. As the conversation went on, the taxi driver said to him, 'I sense that you are not happy. If you believe in Christ it makes all the difference.'

The businessman said to me, 'Here was a man speaking with authority. I thought I was the one in authority. After all, I was paying.' The taxi driver said to him eventually, 'Don't you think it's time you settled all this by accepting Christ?' When they arrived at the airport, the taxi driver said to him, 'Why don't we pray?

If you want Christ in your life, ask him.' They prayed together. That moment changed the whole course of the man's life.

Power

In the New Testament the proclamation of the gospel is often accompanied by a demonstration of the power of God. Jesus came proclaiming: 'The kingdom of God is near. Repent and believe the good news!' (Mark 1:15). Jesus went on to demonstrate the power of the gospel by the expulsion of evil (Mark 1:21–28) and by healing the sick (Mark 1:29–34, 40–45).

Jesus told his disciples to do what he had been doing. He told them to do the works of the kingdom – 'to heal the sick who are there' and to proclaim the good news – and to tell them, 'The kingdom of God is near you' (Luke 10:9). As we read on in the Gospels and Acts we see that this is what they did. Paul wrote to the Thessalonians: 'Our gospel came to you not simply with words, but also with power' (1 Thessalonians 1:5). This was certainly true for me; when I first encountered the power of the Holy Spirit, I experienced what Paul speaks of in Romans 5:5; 'The love of God has been poured out in our hearts by the Holy Spirit who was given to us' (NKJV). Other people testify to the experience of being overwhelmed by the power of the Holy Spirit in terms of the conviction of their sin. When they hear the good news about Jesus, something deeper is going on in their hearts.

Proclamation and demonstration go hand in hand. Often one leads to the other. On one occasion Peter and John were on their way to church. Outside was a man crippled from birth. He had been sitting there for years. He asked for money. Peter said, in effect, 'I am sorry. I haven't got any money, but I will give you what I have. In the name of Jesus Christ of Nazareth, walk.' He took his hand and helped him up. Instantly, he jumped to his feet and began to walk. When he realised he was healed, he leapt and jumped and praised God (Acts 3:1–10).

Everyone knew that this man had been crippled for years, and a huge crowd gathered around. After the demonstration of the power of God came the proclamation of the gospel. People were asking, 'How did this happen?' Peter was able to tell them all about Jesus: 'It is Jesus' name and the faith that comes through him that has given this complete healing to him, as you can all see' (Acts 3:16). In the booklet *Does God Heal Today?* we shall examine this area in more detail by looking at the nature of the kingdom of God and the place of healing within it.

Prayer

We have already seen the importance that prayer had in the life of Jesus. While he was proclaiming and demonstrating the gospel he was also praying (Mark 1:35–37). Prayer is essential in the area of telling others the good news. Similarly, Paul loved people, and out of that love came a desire to pray for them: 'My heart's desire and prayer to God... is that they may be saved' (Romans 10:1).

We need to pray for blind eyes to be opened. Many people are blinded to the gospel (2 Corinthians 4:4). They can see physically, but they cannot see the spiritual world. We need to pray that the Spirit of God will open the eyes of the blind so that they can understand the truth about Jesus.

Most of us find, when we come to faith in Christ, that there has been somebody praying for us. It may be a member of the family, a godparent or a friend. When a friend of mine, Ric, became a Christian he rang a friend whom he knew to be a Christian as well, and told him what had happened. The friend replied, 'I have been praying for you for four years.' Ric then started to pray for one of his own friends, and within ten weeks he too became a Christian.

We need to pray for our friends. We also need to pray for ourselves. When we talk to people about Jesus, we may sometimes get a negative reaction. The temptation at that moment is to give up. When Peter and John healed the crippled man and proclaimed the gospel, they were arrested and threatened with dire consequences should they continue. But they did not give up. Rather, they prayed – for boldness in preaching the gospel and for God to perform more signs and wonders through the name of Jesus (Acts 4:29--31).

It is vital for all of us as Christians to persevere in telling others about Jesus – by our presence, persuasion, proclamation, power and prayer. If we do, over the course of a lifetime we shall see many lives changed.

During the war a man was shot and lay dying in the trenches. A friend leaned over to him and said, 'Is there anything I can do for you?'

He replied, 'No, I am dying.'

'Is there anyone I can send a message to for you?'

'Yes, you can send a message to this man at this address. Tell him that in my last minutes what he taught me as a child is helping me to die.'

The man was his old Sunday school teacher. When the message got back to him, he said, 'God forgive me. I gave up Sunday school teaching years ago because I thought I was getting nowhere. I thought it was no use.'

When we tell people about Jesus, it is never 'no use'. For the gospel 'is the power of God for the salvation of everyone who believes' (Romans 1:16).

Endnotes

1. Bono's speech to the Labour Party Conference, 30 September, 2004; transcript taken from http://news.sky.com/story/294648/bonos-speech-to-labour-full-text

The Jesus Lifestyle   Studies in the Sermon on the Mount showing how Jesus' teaching flies in the face of a modern lifestyle and presents us with a radical alternative.

30 Days   Nicky Gumbel selects thirty passages from the Old and New Testament which can be read over thirty days. It is designed for those on Alpha and others who are interested in beginning to explore the Bible.

All titles are by Nicky Gumbel,
who is vicar of Holy Trinity Brompton

About the Author

Nicky Gumbel is the pioneer of Alpha. He read law at Cambridge and theology at Oxford, practised as a barrister and is now vicar of HTB in London. He is the author of many bestselling books about the Christian faith, including *Questions of Life*, *The Jesus Lifestyle*, *Why Jesus?*, *A Life Worth Living*, *Searching Issues* and *30 Days*.